1 SAMUEL 18—20 FOR CHILDREN

THE SECRET OF THE ARROWS

Written by Alyce Bergey

Illustrated by Jim Roberts

Concordia Publishing House

ARCH Books

COPYRIGHT © 1972 CONCORDIA PUBLISHING HOUSE, ST. LOUIS, MISSOURI

CONCORDIA PUBLISHING HOUSE LTD., LONDON, E. C. 1

MANUFACTURED IN THE UNITED STATES OF AMERICA

ISBN 0-570-06067-2

"You won the battle when you killed
Goliath with your sling!
Brave lad!" cried Saul. But David said,
"God gave me strength, O King."

"From now on you shall lead my men
when they go out to war!
You'll live at court with me," said Saul.
"And you'll tend sheep no more!"

The shy young shepherd
bowed down low.
Beside Saul stood his son.
"Such courage
I have never seen!"
exclaimed Prince Jonathan.

When Saul dismissed them, Jonathan
said, "David, let's be friends."
While late that night the soldiers all
were sleeping in their tents,
the boys still talked — of life at court,
of war and tending sheep.
They promised always to be friends.
At last they fell asleep.

When morning came, King Saul declared,
"We leave for home today."
They broke up camp; then just before
they started on their way,
the prince took off his coat, his sword,
his armor, and his bow.
"They're yours," he said to David.
"Put them on before we go."

Great throngs came out to meet them as
they marched along the way.
Crowds cheered their king as he passed by.
Thought Saul, "My proudest day!"

But when they saw the boy who killed
the giant with his sling,
they cheered him louder — ten times more —
than they had cheered the king!
"Goliath wasn't THAT big — nine —
or maybe ten feet tall,"
the outraged ruler muttered.
"*I'm* the king here, after all."

At last they reached the palace home
where David was to stay.
He tried his best to please the king
in all he did each day.
"Yes, sir!" he said and quickly did
all Saul told him to do.

He played sweet music on his harp
for Saul when day was through.

But nothing pleased the jealous king.
Not one right thing was done.
Saul's anger grew so fierce, one day
he whispered, to his son,
"Kill David when you get a chance."
The prince cried in alarm,
"Please, Father! No! All David does
is good. Don't do him harm!

"You saw him kill Goliath — you
were glad! Why do this thing?"
Saul listened. "David shall not die.
I promise," said the king.

But Saul could not forget the way
the crowds had praised the lad.
"They love him more than me," he thought.
This drove the king quite mad.
He heard the crowds cheer in his dreams
at night as he lay snoring.

All day he sulked — or paced the floor,
raging, raving, roaring!
"What can we do to help the king?"
asked David in dismay.
The prince said, "It may calm him if
you bring your harp and play."

So David played upon his harp
sweet music, soft and clear.
But Saul's face only grew more grim.
His big fist clutched his spear.

Saul hurled it suddenly! He thought,
"I'll pin him to the wall!"
But David dodged and darted out
to flee from furious Saul.

The prince was sad and lonely when
his friend had gone away.
The time passed slowly. "Jonathan!"
a soft voice called one day.

"David!" Jonathan exclaimed.
"Sh-h-h, quiet!" David said.
"Is it safe?" he asked. "Or does
the king still want me dead?"

"We'd better go out to the field,"
suggested Jonathan.
They found a place where they would not
be seen by anyone.

"You hide behind that rock," the prince
told David. "Then just wait.
And I'll find out tomorrow if
the king's still filled with hate.

I'll come here afterward. I'll bring
my arrows and my bow.
The king will think that I intend
to practice when I go.

"I'll shoot three arrows. If I tell
the boy I bring with me,
'The arrows are beyond you,' then
you'll know that you must flee.
But if I say, 'The arrows are
on this side of the rock,'
you'll know my father's wrath is gone.
It will be safe — come back."

Then Jonathan went home again,
and David hid — to wait.

A royal feast was held by Saul
next day. And as he ate,
he noticed David's empty place.
"Where is he?" shouted Saul.
"You hate him. Why?" begged David's friend.
"He's done no wrong at all."

"The people love him more than me!"
Saul stormed. "You foolish son!
You won't be king if David lives!
He MUST die, Jonathan!"

The prince could eat no food; he left
in anger, feeling sad.
Saul threw his spear in fury.
But his aim was very bad.

Prince Jonathan loved David, and
he knew that he must go
to warn his friend; and so he took
his arrows and his bow
and went out to the field. He aimed
and pulled back on the string.
Behind the rock young David heard
three arrows — ping! ping! ping!

Then David heard the arrow boy
the prince brought with him, scurry.
"The arrows are beyond you, lad,"
the prince called. "Don't wait, hurry!"

The boy picked up the arrows.
Said the prince, "That's all today.
Go home, lad." David came out when
the boy had gone away.

The friends were brokenhearted;
their eyes were filled with tears.
They knew they might not meet again
for many, many years.

"You'll be the king someday, my friend,"
said Jonathan, "I know.
Please don't forget me, David, or
my children. Quickly — go!"

"I won't forget you ever, friend,"
said David, filled with sadness;
then left his friend and ran to hide
from Saul's dread hate and madness.

DEAR PARENTS:

Over the years you have learned to value the gift of a friend. One good friend in a lifetime is above the law of averages.

David the shepherd boy and Jonathan the prince enjoyed a friendship that has become a historical model. In this story we see that friendship put to a severe test. Jonathan's father, Saul, the king of Israel, wanted to kill David out of jealousy.

Every friendship demands loyalty. The story of David and Jonathan reminds children of God of another Friend "who sticks closer than a brother." Jesus is such a true friend that He gives His life for His friends. There is no greater love than that.

Impress on your child that friendless as he may be — now or later — he will always be able to count on Jesus as his truest Friend. And he can look for friends among many other people who also have Jesus for their Friend.

Discuss with your child: What is a friend? Children have some profound insights into this relationship. Just talking about it will cause him to think about it.

THE EDITOR